THE
BOOK
OF
JON

BY ELENI SIKELIANOS

CITY LIGHTS • SAN FRANCISCO

Cover design by Yolanda Montijo
Interior design and typography by Yolanda Montijo
Photographs from author's and family's collection

Library of Congress Cataloging-in-Publication Data

Sikelianos, Eleni.
 The Book of Jon : A Memoir / by Eleni Sikelianos.
   p. cm.
 ISBN 0-87286-436-7
 1. Sikelianos, Eleni--Family. 2. Poets, American--20th centu-
ry—Family relationships. 3. Narcotic addicts--United States--
Biography. 4. Homeless persons--United States--Biography. 5.
Fathers and daughters--United States. 6. Greek Americans--
Biography. I. Title.
 PS3569.I4128Z464 2004
 811'.54--dc22

2004008942

City Lights Books are edited by Lawrence Ferlinghetti and
Nancy J. Peters and published at the City Lights Bookstore,
261 Columbus Avenue, San Francisco, CA 94133.

Visit our website: www.citylights.com

This book is for all my tribe, and anyone like them. It is for each of our versions of Jon, for the private version he had of himself, and for that perfect version hanging out somewhere in ideal space, where our most beautiful shadows are cast.

birds with certain wing-load-to-weight ratios, birds who carry
booty in their beaks & birds Black-capped, & air that allows them
Blue-footed, iridescent of the head, slipping through, Herons with
sleeking feathers, who's your father, who? Birds, "My question, answer

in the fewest words,
what sort of life is it
among the children
of the birds?"

Contents

INTRODUCTORY NOTE

This book is part of a longer family history, as of yet
unwritten; a story that embraces morphine and heroin
addicts, refugees, Ionian counts, one of the richest fam-
ilies in the U.S. who exhausted their fortune attempt-
ing to revive the ancient Greek theatre, Lithuanian
Jews, a half dozen musicians, a painter, several poets
(one a Nobel-nominee), a lesbian, opium-runners, wait-
resses, a burlesque dancer called Melena the Leopard
Girl (my maternal grandmother) and a dwarf (one of
her five husbands), all landed, eventually, on the coasts
of our American homeland. It begins in lands and
times we do not know—on Irish isles, on the amber
plains of Anatolia, under the golden light of Attica,
with ship-farers and wags—and snakes through the
early reaches of recorded history on this continent,
runs through Bohemian Europe and America, and
crashes right into the average story of all those happy
hippie plans gone awry.

*

I see the lines of our ancestors laid out in filaments
looping here and there, bifurcating, disappearing;
there are breaks in the thread and dead-ends into the
dark where this or that sister took a boat from Greece
and was lost forever from the fold; men and women who
found each other or for reasons of circumstance were

thrust into each others' arms, radiating out along the great line in pairs; for however much they loved each other or same or other sexes or lived apart, always in this long arrow stretching back to our first humans hunting in the bush somewhere on a far continent in an unfathomable time, it was and is a man and a woman, two-by-two, each representing a small electrical hyphen of human intelligence and endeavor illuminating the path that leads to me sitting here—; men and women, each with eyes lit up for at least one moment in their lives; loving each other in the dark before the advent of writing; or a brief encounter, maybe forced, that led to the continuation of a line; these packets of genes waiting, and that uncontrollable animal urge toward making things—love, babies; the ranks moving forward and forward, branching, fucking, splitting, until they reach the edges of history; and forward, farther, till they hit the periphery of family lore.

Thus begins the tale before human time but in human terms, and stretches far beyond us into a future we cannot imagine, except, perhaps, that it will not contain us as walking libraries. It matters that there are holes in a family history that can never be filled, that there are secrets and mysteries, migrations and invasions and murky blood-lines. These stories speak of human history.

This portion of the tale is about my father, Jon.

ANGELOS SIKELIANOS, GREEK POET —
EVA PALMER SIKELIANOS, AMERICAN THEATER DIRECTOR
| |
GLAFKOS — FRANCES LEFEVRE *(FIRST MARRIAGE)*
| |
MARK

GLAFKOS — MARIAN *(SECOND MARRIAGE)*
| |
CHRIS, JON, MELITSA, POPPY

JON — ELAYNE
| |
ELENI (KID 1, b. 1965)

JON — MERRILL
| |
JOSEF (KID 2, b. 1975)

JON — PAT
| |
EZEKIEL (KID 3, b. 1981), ELYSIA (CALLED POULI) (KID 4, b. 1988)

THE BOOK OF JON

In the evenings, but particularly during the endless lessons at school, I pictured every detail of my future life in America. This period of my imaginary Americanization, during which I crisscrossed the entire United States, now on horseback, now in a dark brown Oldsmobile, peaked between my sixteenth and seventeenth years in an attempt to perfect the mental and physical attitudes of a Hemingway hero, a venture in mimicry that was doomed to failure for various reasons that can easily be imagined.

— W.G. SEBALD

The time of us on earth is spent lightly

on good peas and gravy

good enough for a seconds time

in an hour

—poem by Jon, when he was 18 years old
as transcribed by my mother

Chapter (Dear)

Dear Dad Dear Father Dear Jon Dear Pop,

(This letter is now a part of the story.)

It is mostly a quiet Sunday here in New York—the cats (you have never met them) are lying around or scrabbling in the suitcases in the closet, Laird is in the other room working on his novel, the small voices of children escape from windows across the courtyard and then they rise. Someone outside is banging on something with a hammer; it gives the hour a regular rhythm. It's a grey day here, with a little patch of blue at the top of the sky, and even though it is hazy, I can go out without a jacket—warm for late October.

This morning I woke up with a liquid image of Albuquerque's gridlike streets under a big blue autumn sky, cedar smoke rising and filling the neighborhood with the smell of the highlands, mixing with the whiter clouds, the Sandias laid out and also rising in that luminous watermelony-and-gold light. The neighbors are so quiet there. I think of the times I walked down Marble or Lead with you or Zeke or Pouli, the only sound our feet scuffling up leaves, or our voices shot up though the breakable, crystalline air.

When did I see you last?

In March, I think there was snow, and you were not well.

5

The first day, we had a good talk in Pat's backyard, you crouching, me sitting in the hard-crusted dirt, the sun warming our shoulders. I can hardly remember what we talked about—books, maybe. And then the talk turned to guns—the variety and nature of each you had investigated and examined or had pointed at you recently. You had a job to do and we walked through the quiet streets of your old neighborhood (you had wrecked your truck a month earlier and were wheeling a bicycle along with your left hand) and on through other neighborhoods, past little dry plots of sandy dust that stood for yards, past medians, barking dogs and all manner of crocuses poking up from the dirt, till we reached the site. The owners of the house invited us in for tea and toast, they had just moved from Chicago, their son lived in Baltimore. The woman was painting burgundy- and cream-colored squares onto the kitchen floor. Houses were much cheaper here, she said, and needed a lot of work. They had a tree down, but they had a lot to talk about, and you didn't work that day.

The next time I saw you that trip, you were drunk or high, and babbled about your recent love interest, and your half-cracked entrepreneurial schemes. I didn't want to hear about it, and for the first time, I told you. Then you were excited about the prospect of seeing me read, because you thought maybe I would stop in the middle and say to the audience, And there is my father, pointing, and all the good-looking women in the room would turn to you like luscious, trembling flowers to a dark, underwater sun, and smile. But you did not make it the fifty miles to Santa Fe.

I have never thought of you as part of any trend—just as a human out there, sometimes gone missing in the desert, sometimes out of his cracked mind, a person whose spinning thoughts could never be predicted or duplicated—but here you are, part of a long, boring trend of absent fathers and junk-high assholes.

Pat tells me you lost your apartment. You are living near a dumpster off University. You O.D. at regular intervals, have grand mal seizures, get beat up with crow bars, have your wallets stolen, come down with pneumonia. There must be a black hole out there somewhere near your pocket sucking up keys and good sense, trucks, tools and cash.

As a child, the few times I saw you, I gloried in the hours when you pounded out songs on the piano, told stories about dogs or cats you'd known, about pulling a piece of paint off Rousseau's painting in the Louvre when you were 16 and keeping that morsel in your pocket all summer, fingering it till there was nothing left but powder. I have seen you falling asleep under that fixed blue sky, with those black lions. I have never —I suppose it is particular to sons or daughters—really thought you were going to die. In a hotel room, soon, with a shoelace strapped onto your biceps, or tumbling down a long flight of stairs with your brain in a quivering yellow seizure. That your blood might freeze into icy clumps one of these winter nights, that you won't get your methadone, that the final pneumonia will sneak over you come dawn. That you will become so stupid you're not worth talking to, and there will be the ongoing endeavor to remember the old Pops, on his best nights. I have no hopes of you meeting grandchildren, or seeing my sister into adulthood.

There are the factors: a chemical predisposition, habit, availability, weakness of will—but I cannot fathom how your life has continued to be so dissolute. You have fallen apart, you have recovered, fallen apart. In the white snowy towns of your youth, in the brutality of American families and lawn-filled landscapes, with the blue winter light opening over you—how will you survive?

I am sending this letter on to Pat, in hopes that she will find you.

Notes Towards a Film About My Father
(Jon)

WORDS (WHITE) ARE FLASHED QUICKLY ON A BLACK SCREEN IN RHYTHMIC SEGMENTS:

This is a film about my father / with no pictures
Why should I make a movie / of him? /
It's true / I probably love him / more than you do, / and it's
funny / that this is based simply on the fact / that he's my
dad. / It's possible / it's been known to happen / this could
have made me love him / less. / I repeat: / Why should I
make a film / about my father, / and one without / images? /
Because a movie would not be able to show /
all the representations / of why I love him. /
It might be impossible to tell / why / from likenesses. /
Why? /
Because he looks like me? / (I mean / I / look like him. /
We used to. / Before he got / old and /
craggy.) Because we both wear Levi's? / (Although / I only do /
sometimes.) / (pause.) / There is something / you should know /
about my father and me. /
I didn't see him much / between the ages / of six months /
and thirteen. / My father taught me / how to drive /
but I slammed on the brakes / too hard / and almost broke /
my brother's nose. / I saw my father / approximately / once
a year / after that. / Maybe you know this /
story? /

9

To repeat / an unrepeated answer / trying to respond / to the question: / Why should I make a movie about / Jon? /

Because some humans / will go / and what will be / left of them? / (pause.) / No. / Because / I love him / (Jon). /

Now there is the real movie, with real pictures. These happen in intervals. Some minutes (unspecified) of footage of my father, then no pictures, but word-intervals again. Maybe in 24 segments. It might take me until his death to finish this project.

Some shots I would like to show:

Jon playing the piano.
Jon lighting a cigarette (that's easy).

Although my father / was a heroin addict / for twenty / years or so, we probably won't / show / this / picture.

Jon / is shy / about a camera / and that's like a chapter / in this / story. /

5 sentences

Date Unknown

Seen from the air, across this valley floor: fields of light, Everglades of swampy light, light in runnels, ruins of lights crumbling, lights like shining asters melting at the edges, vagrant starlike pinpoints winking from the foothills; mountains, explosions of highways of liquid lights like floral antechamber arrangements detonating in lowlands below; lights informally or formally seeded across a plain, a glade of some dusty green, dusty blue, amber, some red, some white. And when a lake, no lights; just darkness, and silence. And then lights again, amber and white, stuttering. Each light is a thought, a thought goes out. Each light a string, a web of thoughts, persons/people thinking in the dark making thoughts shine and knit and spin under a bulb of light; or the dark-thoughted feet shuffling from room to room, over rough wooden floors, a hand moving across plaster and dry wall, shooting around molding, door jamb, to unhinge a door, to break the light bulb, plunged into my father's dark world; Albuquerque.

A knot of thought at the forehead. It's me trying to remember not the events but the scenery and sounds that unfold to make up the last visit with my father. And the lights laid out, as one descends upon the scene.

Little spheres of blood on the piano keys, then a head banging down, a face presses into the keys and stays

11

there, dried leaf in thinning hair. Frizzled brown leaf, frizzled brown hair. A line of spittle makes its slow saga onto the keys. The head does not move, not for a long while. It is framed by two hands with gnarled knuckles, blunt at the extremities, torn fingernails, dressed in scabs caused by the disease, the fingers still in the shape of a beautiful chord they have made on the piano.

In this life, there were supermarket scenes among the coffee cake and frozen peas.

The Duke of Albuquerque

There is my father
in the doorway. What is he

doing there?
He stands. He happens

again and again. I happen
to be here, where my father is

tonight, standing in the door-
way. I happen to be trying to fit him in

to the size of this room.

There are his shoes.
What are they doing?

There are his hands, little
scabs. There is his

nose, but
disappearing. My father
disappears in the frame of
the door

frame like a black

pinhole that starts here & then grows
to his specifications (skeletal).
There is a thick
black heavy black

space made in his shoulders'
frame & then he is

here he is again, trying

to fit into the room with
clothespins, kitchen table, hills, pastel colored
pencils, dust
clumps, & pillows. He puts his

head down on pillows. His thinking
is clouding, like the clouded

leopard paces curved
lines around the edges of caves & is
restless in short stubby

legs & beautiful
tail in the terrible

zoo, Albuquerque. His spots
are nebulous, floating through
and over his soft grey

cloudy silk made for animals, not
hats. He is alone tonight but from this
cage he can hear the lion *(Panthera
leo)* roar in the stucco
boat cave. My father *(Pater mia)* from his house
on Lead heard it when he lived there, he has the
same blood

disease as King George, it's making him
mad & gives you scabs

on your hands. He is moving his
hands back through the black

frame, night erasing the downy black
doorway, hands

disappearing, appearing
& gin, whiskey, anything his liquid
pocket is all liquid his hands

liquefying in all
liquidness, the night
my father
stood framed in the door of excess, like
40 milligrams & cigarettes
impressed with the fast
liquefaction of this fleshly

dress. Father, my hand versus
your mouth,   my fist,   wrist,
your smoke cloud, which has more

to say, rope bruises
to the neck? A bird of my tongue

and a beast
of yours, the body

of your discourse is guarded
in fragments, small doses
glued at the hem, basted on neither
your tongue nor your word

sun nor your sun
light. Sometimes lemonade is square and a square can
prick a tongue, but yours is more
brambly.   A plaid

shirt versus the evening you took my brother
too far down the detergent aisle at

Landmark. This is where we
walk & talk, in the frozen foods section
with fur collars on. We're getting every thing
straightened

out. Potatoes, peas, our livers are
getting all fixed up, carrots.

The dark marks
all over this scene

are shadows; shadows are agencies
for eyes to know a world
has shape. We move

between colors. From seeing, I learned theft &

fraud, blue can
fake a blue.

So thanks for the blueberry pie, Pops,
but you took half of it home with you!
You cheated at *tres quatro cinco seis!*
Stole peaches from Landmark!
Your teeth which are henceforth
reduced to broken stubs in the gum &
forests, forests, now

shush. Please exit
the frame using the leg body leg
method and keep the oxygen
levels steady.

When the light printed on my silver
gut, & what
it did: it unspun &
spelled (this doorframe) back-
wards.

If I had my mouth, I would bite; if I
had my liberty I would go walking
with a good leg, and a good foot
and enough money in my purse

Here, wait, let's dance out the answer.

A Few Stories with Jon and Elayne,
as told by Elayne

1. My dad goes to a party. I am not born yet, but my mom
    is there. "My Ming vase," says the girl throwing the
    party, "my Botticelli. Out, all of you, get out!" My dad
    gets mad and crumbles potato chips over her head. Is
    this really true, I ask? It sounds like a 50s movie (*The
    Wild Ones*). It's really true, my mom says. The girl
    calls the cops. In the 60s, you can get arrested for
    crumbling potato chips over peoples' heads. The cops
    arrive. Don't run, my mom says. He runs. They catch
    him. And his brother too. Do you know who we are,
    they yell. My mom laughs, but says, please don't hurt
    him. So they arrest her too. In jail, they feed her a
    bologna sandwich with mustard for dinner. The next
    day, the paper reads, "and the girlfriend was arrested
    when she jumped into the fray."

2. When they are courting, they cruise up to Mountain
    Drive with cold, bottled cokes and Uno bars to watch
    the sunset. Often, they fall asleep in the car and wake
    up to see the sun rise, too.

3. There is an earthquake. A fairly big one, as California
    is wont to have. But no one is hurt, nothing terribly
    broken. A man has been thrown from his deck and is
    sitting on a lawn rubbing his head. "All I've ever
    worked for! Everything! All I've ever worked for," he
    keeps saying and rubbing his head. (My father, who

walked by this scene, gets home to the little house on Prospect Street and tells my mother the story.)

4. Jon and Elayne have a fight because Elayne has been flirting with her old boyfriend, Joe Campos. While Jon was out, Joe Campos came over to try to cure me of colic. Joe rubbed a tablespoon of warm olive oil on my belly and wrapped me in cotton. (I stopped crying.) "Wha-at?!" says Jon. Elayne throws Jon's stuffed bear into the fireplace. He bends all her spoons and one by one lays them on the bed in their tiny room.

5. Later, Joe Campos teaches Jon how to climb and trim trees. Many years later Joe tells Elayne, "Jon hated to work more than any man I ever met. One day we were up in a tree and Jon looked down at the ground and said to me, 'Joe, I wish I would fall out of this tree right now and break my legs so I wouldn't have to work all week. I would just stay home and play guitar all day.'"

Date Unknown

We waited four days for him to come over. The first day he didn't call because he said he didn't know we were there already, the second day he called and said he would come but did not, the third day he came at ten in the morning while I was in the shower, soap in my hair, and wanted me to get out immediately, he had to leave in eighteen minutes.

When he lived there it was a house in perpetual motion. Jon walking out the backdoor slamming the screen. Jon angling through the kitchen, knees bent, arms turned slightly outward, hands large and making more motion than is necessary for simple walking, the whole torso torqued to the side. His body, a study in corkscrewed angles. Or not the body, but how he has trained the muscles to move and hold and handle it, bone and nail and shoulder and tooth. The full wrapper askew, the contents maybe (maybe not) fixable. Jon, leaving a bowl of oatmeal to make a phone call but instead banging out the front door or the back and will he come home in one hour, in twelve, in three? He has forgotten. Forgotten what he was doing and puts on the glasses with one black arm missing, mutters over the dictionary/encyclopedia reading the entries for hours. Or the History Channel: old men are moving against a grey field that once was green. They have been speaking of war, of things that happened many years before, of standing upright in foxholes for 48 hours, huddled together, teeth rattling in winter air.

Then he is still. The oatmeal rallying into a cold, gooey lump in the green plastic bowl by the telephone book. What comes next?

Shreds of stories:

Sawed-off shotgun with a pistol trigger. Crowd-pleaser. Eight-rounder, .357 with expanding bullets, spit-polished gunmetal, buckshot for the first two rounds so that if your hands are shaking side to side—or up and down or whatever, but shaking bad—you can still hit if not kill your target. Nigel came in high and waving it around, Jon in the bedroom with Nigel's girlfriend, although nothing was going on. Hey, nothing's going on, man. I-swear-to-god, nothing, no-thing. Comprende?

Jon knows a guy, Vince, who drove him up over the mountains past Madrid, who killed at least seven civilians: one woman, a girl he thought had a grenade strapped to her abdomen, an old man plowing a field with a water buffalo . . . I bet you don't have the guts to kill that guy, I bet you can't hit him from here, someone said, so Vince used his head for target practice.

Tell me a story about the war.
All right, six lines, no child should hear more.

The dark story has come to an end and will resurface from its pool only briefly this evening, in the kitchen.

—Is Vanessa here? I want to show her my gun.

These were not his stories, but stories he picked up along the way, on the street, in hotel rooms with strangers, men and women with whom he spent an afternoon then an evening then a dawn in the perfect intimacy of a high, and never saw again—every story told with a gush of deathless kinship—two human points have intersected tonight, however messy the tub of guts may be.

No choos! Un hombre muy malo
sin zapatos!

The snow is piling up. It's flying little white blind spots across the air and landing in soft, silky layers. It is pillowing the earth, a featherbed to end all rust and dirt. Trees hope to shake free of the white glove, but won't. A man walks through the window, walking through snow. He is wearing moccasins or he is barefoot. He walks all day and he walks all night over the small foothills through the scrub brush and the snow and sometimes he runs. He runs or he walks, just for the fuck of it. The dark night around him howling, or the day laid out brightly over the sky.

[Picture here of me & Jon, Jon: wild hair; me: 15]

He thinks he will walk all the way to Santa Fe but does not because this is several years later—many years later, to be accurate. And he is tired now of walking all night, all day, he doesn't do that anymore but he will speak of it as if he will—"I will go out and walk all night in the goddamned moonlight, I'll walk all the way to Santa Fe in the snow just for the fuck of it."

Now the snow has melted; light splaying across sage brush, an impossible green, light leaving Mt. Bianco in darkness but draping itself over spike-needled leaves and woody stems and soft brown dirt—as if light loved the ground more than the heights.

They French kiss for five seconds on the bed, she pulls his hands onto her breasts, and he is sure—what is he sure of? It's a hotel room, pea-green blanket on the bed, one chest-level rectangular window running across the wall, white stucco foam on the ceiling with glitter like shimmery, minuscule stars. A pressboard nightstand and wobbly chair, the door at his back, and outside, the cold starry night, New Mexico, and its meridians.

When he was twenty, that kid O.D.'d out in Texas, and they felt compelled to drive his body back to Wyoming. What was his name? Ricky? Eddie? Boy? Like his grandfather, Jon thought if he lay on the body long enough his own body heat (he had heat to spare) might bring the boy back to life. And like his grandfather, in a famous story involving several days and a dead mailman, no one was revived, though a small stench started up, and I never heard if they ditched the body or did, for once, make it all the way to Wyoming. Or this is a story Jon told me really happened, but I begin to wonder if he'd watched too many movies. The overdosed friend ash-lipped, pale face like a nighttime sky with a winter moon spreading in its midst.

This was back in the days when you could still get lost in Juarez and kick up the dust when the light came down slant-long and yellow on the surface of the dusty earth and you could walk in the open hours of evening in boots even in American towns and some of the alleys were still dirt and you could walk without another body gumming up the works.

Supermarket, 1968

It is the year of the student revolution in France. Elayne and I are in a supermarket in Santa Barbara, maybe getting some bananas, which I will later ask her to cut "like that" (waving my hand in the air in several directions), and will cry when she doesn't understand what I still know to have meant lengthwise, and the tears are tears of frustration at not having enough language to say what I mean. A man my mother seems to know approaches. He's wearing loose-fitting Levi's, dirty on the thighs, frizzled hair with twigs in it. I hide behind her legs while they talk, one arm around her left knee. He goes away.

Date Unknown

Houses and houses and houses and houses. Houses and houses and houses and a pool. Then the bigger buildings rise up out of the Earth's surface at the radiating axis of the city. Cars move around, people inside them. (Watch) from the window as the city changes from a sea of houses laid out in sloppy grids, splattered across the valley, creeping into the mountains, falling off into the sea. (But there is no sea here.)

— Is this your inch? Whose inch is this? I will build a house on it.

Watch as the city shrinks from the window, into this specific patch of grass, that roof, those antennae, that language, that garage, a driveway, a child on a Big Wheel. The child has shiny hair. It's not a Big Wheel, it's a Hippity-Hop; she bounces down the driveway and into Carpinteria, 1970.

There are hobos out by the traintracks they wear bandannas over their chins and noses when the train stops they jump off chickencoop roofs and trains the children playing in the sandpit by the line of eucalyptus trees scream, men in dark stubble jump off the train to scare them, children of shiny hair, that is their job, to scare them, although they never jump off, the children never see them the children jump up from the sandpit screaming and run when the train stops. This is at dusk, and the night-towering lemon is where we hide.

Because I have abandoned many things—lovers, hou
hours, cats, cities—I hate to leave. I hate to leave restau-
rants, I hate to leave parties, I hate to leave the house
after breakfast. But I am always willing to leave a lover
or a city or a friend or my father, if not for good.

Later, just me, arriving in a border town long after dark in
a country far from here, or on the outskirts of the capital,
the train pulls in, we sling our packs onto our backs; night;
bushes. Where do you sleep in dusty Khartoum?

As a young man, my father crisscrossed this country so
many times a small constellation appeared, a light board
with half-aborted destinations; he left barely visible elec-
trical lines tracing and flashing after him, like the small
luminous dots that line the sides of some fish, to help them
keep their bearings. I chose to travel to distant countries,
where no buses could be found, no telephones, and by the
time I got home, you could not drag my father twenty min-
utes away from home to go to the movies.

Here is a journey.

The diner a buy-one-dinner-get-the-second-free kind
of place, the rancid odors of badly mopped floors, wet rags
and old grease, brown crumbs of ancient hamburgers lit-
tering the grill, and of course it's run by a Greek, one
Kostas, from Chios. My grandfather was a very important
poet in Greece, he was the stuff. Yeah, yeah, and my
father was a Turk. Jon asks for the ticket, one-way to NY,

hands over his seven dollars then eyes the waitresses. Tired creatures with skinny, flabby legs, knees knobbing through thick stockings, busy leaning on the counter smoking, calling everybody "Hon." "Hon" this and "Hon" that, "What'll you have, Hon?" "Do you want more hot water, Hon?" "Sure, Hon." "I'll be right back with that, Hon." "Hon, I'll bring you sommore hon." Don't these people know about the greatest invader in history? One Attila. A blond with dark roots, hair pulled tight into a ponytail that will not smooth the mildly craggy folds of her face, is busy saying something about her daughter. She lowers her voice in confidentiality, a boyfriend is involved, a scar hovers on the bone below her right oculus, moving up to the subtle arrow of her eye. The scar wriggles as she talks. The other waitress makes a quick glancing movement toward Jon with a lower-your-voice we've-got-a-listener look and Jon wants to smack her, pop her right in the face, for being so stupid, so ugly, for working in this stinking diner with rotten coffee run by a stinking Greek who doesn't know a shit's worth about his own country's poetry. *Ena potiri skata, parakalo.* A glass of shit, please. Prince So-and-So taught me how to ask for a glass of shit. How do you say I want a glass of water? *Ena potiri skata.* A glass of shit. The waiter looks at him, bemused. You crazy Americans. You would have me ask for a glass of shit, you A-rab Prince? Yes. Oh, yes.

The slow or fast slide into degeneracy, what caused it? From childlike innocence to now.

After the house burned down, my grandfather Glafkos and

his second wife Marian packed their four children, two cats, one dog and a parakeet into a jeep and took off from Cape Cod across America to find the right place to live. A few months later they settled in a small town in California by the sea, where they wrecked cars and threw glasses at each other, and a few years later Marian packed up their trunks and took the kids to drive across Europe looking for the right place to live. Their children played poker in the car, learned how to pluck out a few tunes on the guitar. In Greece, they were befriended by a farmer's son and an Ottoman prince, basking in the fame of their grandfather-poet. They rented an apartment in Psychiko, and for months slept on the floors with not a single trace of furniture in any room. Melitsa, the girl, wore a pea-coat through the Athenian summer; the first signs of her madness had appeared. It was clear that Greece was not the right place to live. In Montreaux, on the shores of lake Geneva, they watched the ducks float by and learned a few words in French. Ah, oui, ahx non, my father mouthed. They skied a little and marveled at the bright shops lining the streets, pointing at the unplucked chickens hanging in the window; they went to school for a month or two, but it was not the right place to live. In all their looking for the right place to live my grandfather's children found some wrong ways to live.

None of these stories will stitch up into a seamless blanket to cover this family's tracks. In this story, all the fissures show, they bulge scarlike, they come apart at the seams or they were never sewn up in the first place. This thread (my father's life at fifteen in Lausanne), that thread (my grandfather's life at sixteen in Delphi), unravel and twist, the snaking lines of those beautifully colored cartographer's maps coming unhinged from their borders and uncoiling away off the page, disappearing into the aethers. There is nothing left on the map, just some names here and there, and swathes of color.

Jon pulls his agitated electricities back into himself, tensing all his muscles, and bursts into the sunlight. He smokes six cigarettes sitting on the steps of the ticket office before the bus pulls in.

At Albany, he spends his twenty-five minutes walking the blocks around the bus depot, a huge elaborate stone castle nearby, once the seat of New York government. He buys a fresh pack of smokes at the newsstand, a crisp blue day, his legs taking in the concrete in long rubbery strides, a few stiff-legged men sitting in doorways of old brick buildings in alleyways. He finds a bookstore marked BOOK-STORE, used paperbacks in bins out front; inside, that fantastically musty smell of ruined books. "Can I help you?" a fat faggy man emerges from behind the dust-laden stacks. The front corridor lined with piles of *Playboys, Hustlers,* Jon's eyes glaze past them and he glides into the farther rooms. In ten minutes, he finds Vol. I of *La Comédie Humaine*, no. 80 stamped in red in an edition of one thousand (which he will quickly become bored with and abandon on the bus), buys it for a nickel, and makes with the goods back toward the bus utterly pleased with himself as he swallows up these four square blocks of an unfamiliar city, in the warm April sunlight, and time to smoke two more Camels.

It does not occur to him that his daughter might make this same journey, thirty-odd years later stopping in Albany at the bus depot, the same bookstore with the same, older, owner; that she will sit down under the vertical bus stop sign, a box for each letter: B U S D E P O T in greying print, and on the side, two characters to a box: "cocktails, snacks," as if somebody might actually come here not to get the bus, but for cocktails, snacks; he is nineteen and it does not perhaps occur to him, even, that he has a daughter; but he does, a nine-month-old daughter on the other side of that long great place which was once Maine-Alaska.

The bus stinks of swilled toilet chemicals and wet t.p. and shit and sweaty men. It rolls into the parking lot one minute behind schedule. Our driver has white hair and a yellowing mustache, a slim man, just under six foot, who lost eighty pounds last year on a no-fat diet. He's of Irish extraction and hates tea. At loading time he cheerfully trundles us on board. "I guess we can arrange for you all to get to New York City. Got your lunch bags?" he says looking into the rearview mirror. He makes this trip once a week, NYC to Montreal, Montreal to NYC. If he sees Earl driving the Dog in the opposite direction at Saratoga Springs at 11:40 instead of at Keane at 11:15, he know the road conditions are bad. If he sees Max near Cats' at 12:56, he knows the traffic's backed up. A secr from Queens sits in the seat behind him and gat prostitutes, rapes, murder. Mmhmm, he says, I see. I agree with you there, Ma'am, he says. Two older Quebequoises ladies in stretch pants and t-shirts have long discussions about the merits of _____ in Canuck-y French. A Sikh in a bright red turban sits with his hands folded in his lap, and whips out his cell phone at every stop. A Jamaican woman and her granddaughter, about whom she occasionally says, "That child!", sit quietly eating potato chips. It is a morning bus and the riders are slow and quiet and sleepy, half-witted in the early sunlight, some of them on since Montreal, where they woke up in the dark and made it in due time to the depot only to wait in bus terminal chairs for hours. A Panamanian couple, the one college student (a young Black man on his way down to the city from Skidmore), a Midwestern woman with grey hair, a representative collection of my countrymen and women, my history.

What is it I want from this story? What do I want to have happen in it? My father stops being a bum, straightens up and flies right, gets a blue-and-white-striped shirt and gives up heroin. He gets a job at a zoo, and he loves it. My mother loses sixty pounds, stops telling the same stories over and over except when I want to hear them, and goes ⌐ol. They both get a load of money, with no ⌐ry involved (an occasional lie is houses in beautiful towns far away ⌐ne, but I can go there on holidays and ⌐nny beach nearby, or a pristine mead- ⌐nlit cliffs with fat-ass purply butterflies flitting slowly around. My mother is never irritating, she has learned to cook, and we sail to the Galapagos for Christmas. She has given away her vast collection of untouched sewing projects. Ha ha. In this story, my father did come to see me every week when I was a child, and took me to the races, and we shot rocks at tin barrels in nearby streams and I always hit the target with a resounding, soul-satisfying *thwunk!,* and he told me the stories of when he was a child, so that I knew the names of his dogs, his peeves, his adventures and his loves.

Billy the Kid

I think I must be eleven. Maybe I am thirteen. My father has taken me somewhere—why? I mean, why am I with him? It must be the time my mother was in the hospital with her second tubular pregnancy; the father would have been Carl, I think; an unborn half brother or sister.

Where he has taken me is a bar. Why I'm allowed in I cannot say, except that it's the 70s, when nearly everything was possible if you weren't in Vietnam. And even there. Although the war must have been over by now. I think I was nine.

The truth of the matter is I hardly know my father, as it always has been, as it always will be. He would cry if he read that sentence. As I am crying as I write it . Because I am listening to the song that I'm trying to write about.

We're in the bar, he's trying to teach me to play pool. I have a streak of beginner's luck, as it turns out I often do —five balls pocketed in one round. (The first time I throw a bowling ball, a perfect strike, but I never hit another pin again.)

He (Pop? Dad? Jon? what to call him?) sends me over to the jukebox to see if there's anything I like. I come back, lean in near him. Yeah, there's this song I kind of like. He gives me a quarter. And in retrospect I remember somehow knowing it would please him, and that this is part of why, in that moment, it was a song I liked.

In the movie for which the song seems to have been written, and which I watched a few years ago, Kris Kristofferson plays the part of Billy the Kid.

Trees

This one's a golden chinquapin, and that one's a sycamore. All the Santa Barbara oaks have a heart-rotting disease. (We're driving through one of the canyons.) There's black oaks, live oak—the coastal , the canyon, and the interior oak —blue oak, valley oak. Did you know they're in the beech family? Genus *Quercus.* That's from Celtic, even though it's Latin now, for "fine" and "tree." A fine tree, the oak. All those men and women turning into trees, like Cyparissus, do you know that story? whose hair grew straight up toward heaven after he accidentally shot his favorite deer.

The lazy raging maw of the chainsaw growling through limbs and trunks. I, Eleni, fried my ankle on the exhaust once. The men, my father, shouting Hoa! into the sunlight as the toothed metal eats through wood. Then the murderous chthonic crash, the rumble as houses jolt and settle back into bentonite.

He couldn't learn to stand still and look quietly but could sometimes stand still and look quietly, sideways, at a girl.

I can lay on the ground and feel we are a part of things— but *what* things? The grass, the trees, the sky? I spent most of my life not knowing people. Not knowing my father, my brother, my next brother, my sister. Spread out across great distances of time and space and communication devices. What apparatus will teach us to learn to know each other? I know this landscape in my memory: a girl, a woman, turns into a tree, a madrone in the hills above town that breaks into blossom, as was planned, each spring.

But these *are* the people we know, however badly we know them.

he Touch

My father has what people in the industry call "the touch."
How he developed it I don't know. If it's genetic, I'm un-
aware of its presence—but I've never been offered a clear
opportunity to find out if I too have it. The touch mani-
fests in this way: my father understands bears, and bears
understand him.

Some Things My Father and His Brothers Know About Animals

They know that seals are pinnipeds, fin-footed animals that once crawled onto land, became bearlike, then crawled back into the sea again.

My father knows about coatimundis, and likes to talk about them, savoring each syllable of the word. Coatimundi (*Nasua nasua* or *Nasua narica*), an omnivorous, tree-dwelling relative of the raccoon. "Ko WAH ti MUN dees" he says, "poke their leetle snouts under rocks looking for beetles, grubs, worms, ants, termites, scorpions, centipedes, juicy insects, leetle mammals, fat amphibians, dee-licious arthropods." "A KoWAHtiMUNdee," he says, "has highly sensitive feet, a veery long tail for balance in a tree, eminently flexible ankles, so he can patter headfirst down that tree. He might move his leetle snout in leetle circles, walking along a branch, snuffing the air. When they talk, they talk in a chirp chirp chirp, just like an African thumb harp. When they walk, they keep their tails nearly perfectly straight, just a leetle curl, for sauciness, at the tip."

He gets up for a cup of coffee. He comes back. There is more to say about coatimundis. He's serious now.

Social animals, with a range from Big Bend, Texas (where they are called hog-nosed coons) all the way down to Argentina, they live in groups of 15 to 20. During the night, they sleep in treetops in nests of leaves.

Zoo Stories

1. When I was very small, my father worked at the Childs Estate Zoo. He brought back a fox for me to watch for a few days. My mother claims I put my face right up to the cage and never flinched, even when it tried to snap through the bars. When I was a little older, and I hardly knew him, he'd sometimes come over with Suzie the chimp slung over his hip, which terrified me since Suzie didn't like women or girls, human or monkey, and screamed whenever she saw one.

   Years later, when he no longer worked at the Childs Estate, sometimes we'd go to the zoo and there was Suzie, an old friend of my absent father, swinging in her big tire, or racing around her cage.

2. Nights, he might take his keys and go swimming with the seals in an old holding pool that had windows in it for children to see the shadowy black shapes sliding through the water.

3. There was, for example, Boufa the Bear, an old Russian Bear at the zoo in New Hampshire, with whom my father used to drive around. Boufa would clamber into the zoo cart, and off they'd go on their rounds. Boufa had big tufts of hair on his cheeks, my father liked to say when I was grown, and he'd gesture a big bouffy moustache-shaped thing in the air.

Story

There is no one in this world stronger than my father. His
muscles are gleaming. They are the brightest point in the
universe, glowing out
towards the poles over a dark figure of
globe. These are the muscles in the small triangle
that would be the spiritual
muscle. The coordinates of the
spiritual muscle exert a certain pressure over
everyday objects. He puts things in different,
difficult orders. He places things in his
spiritual muscle (fluids). My father's arm
gives me a headache. I
hear it at night. At night I hear the clinking
of the teaspoon in the tea
cup in the spiritual triangle in my father's

spiritual arm. Steps
below stairs, the creaking
of windows or doors. Someone
is mixing
honey in. In my father's
arm is this sweet stuff and tea and the love of a spoon, a
string, tourniquet.
In his arm is the Bermuda Triangle. In my father's spiritual arm in the dark is the dark he is worried about the
starving elm beetles. In my father's spiritual arm is a picture of me when I was a baby I have a soft skull, he is kissing it. In the middle of my father's spiritual arm are light
snow flurries, barely visible now, and little drops of blood
on the piano keys.

List of Stories to Add

1. What good is Methadone? A government subplot? (No high, but hard on the body. Who manufactures it?)
2. Hiding all the prescriptions when he comes over
3. Burnt spoons in the drawer
4. Taking Melitsa's Haldol (an antipsychotic, for schizophrenia) then jumping on a motorcycle (his arms wouldn't work)
5. Sparky the "High Class Prostitute" (a crack whore missing nearly every tooth in her head, who probably killed her husband—his car was found at the end of a long dirt road—) lurching around the living room
6. The unfinished homemade tattoo he later cut out himself
7. Laird's mock parable "Ark"; "Goddamn," Jon said, "I can't believe we know the guy who wrote that."

    Here is another version. Just as the conception of the Ark was pinioned on sets of two, so, like the image in a slightly warped mirror, there was another Noah, one who had also built a fine enough ship at God's bidding, only to his ark no animals came. Nor did wife or child come and when he searched the hills and dales he found that all those he had known and loved in his life had vanished

    is how the piece begins

8. Pop asked, "Do you mean is Johnny Cash a real guy? Yeah, he's a real guy"
9. The family that frays together (does what?) together

10. Laird and I were supposed to meet Pop, Pat, Zeke, Pouli out on the land, but couldn't rent a car (no credit card, no driver's license) to get there. Finally got there; found a warm spot where their fire had been

11. "The Rolling Stones mean so much to me" (looks at Laird out of the corner of his eye; Mick Jagger is screaming into a microphone on TV; it's a joke)

12. Blind pianist down the street who showed us "shake" and "spear" in the King James, psalm 46 (count down 46, and, omitting the closing *Selah*, up 46 words) as evidence of Shakespeare writing himself in where he could. "*Though* the waters thereof roar *and* be troubled, *though* the mountains shake . . ." All this while Laird was being tied up by my siblings (Pouli: five, Zeke: twelve), who were lighting up cigarettes, pretending to smoke, and playing War, then doing a war dance around Laird's chair (who was of course only pretending he couldn't get free)

13. Drinking a cockroach at the Lead Street house

14. Paisanos—*Tortilla Flats*—maybe all Pop wanted to be was a paisano

15. Poison oak on the backs of my knees from sitting on Pop's lap when he came to see us in the trailer park on Salinas Street. I was six, and so excited to see him I jumped on my new bike and rode it through the gravel without help for the first time. That Christmas he gave me the red Leadbelly '78 ("All the children get so happy / on a Christ – mas day // All the children run and tell their pappy / on a Christ – mas day")

16. Mysterious Switzerland

17. Jon, always writing phone numbers in pencil on the wall

18. Cupping a cigarette in his hand
19. Taking him some silverware on Bath Street when I was 11—I worried he'd have no utensils with which to eat
20. Teaching him The Pretzel in his apartment by the beach (we stood on the bed so no one would get hurt)
21. Pop, I forgot to tell you, Robert Johnson's guitar is threatening your life, Lightnin' Hopkins' is sweet
22. "Giant Squid . . . Attack Not Often," said little brother Joe in his sleep
23. "You look better without all that stuff on your face," said Jon when he took me to school for the first time in his life (I was 13, more worried about being seen in the beat-up Nova he was driving)
24. How to explain it? As he exited a room, he'd briefly place his hand on the tops of our heads—all the feeling (waves of heat) that pulsed through his palm
25. Of my first book of poems, he said, "It's like an excited kid doing brodies in the dirt" (a brody is a figure-eight)

The Trip

My father and his girlfriend decide to kick H. They have spent the $20,000 or so he got on an injury settlement in one short year, and so it seems a good time to take a vacation, a trip across the country, to move 3,000 miles away, leave their habitat/habit behind, to take their young son and drive, to invite Jon's older children along for the ride, to hitch a trailer to an old rusting Chevy pickup with an engine that can barely haul brush and to caravan across California, Nevada, Arizona, New Mexico, Colorado, to "the land."

My father picks me up from the fancy house in Montecito where I have a job as a live-in housekeeper/cook in exchange for a room. I'm eighteen. My brother Joe (eight) is waiting with Pat and Zeke (three) in a Safeway parking lot downtown with the trailer packed with stuff and the littler car. (Pouli is not yet born.) Pat and Jon spend an hour trying to hitch the trailer to the Chevy. They spend several more in Safeway. It's dusk, and we get started, Pop, me and Joe in the cab of the Chevy, Pat and Zeke following in the Honda.

Several days seem to pass.

Nevada; the truck breaks down. It gets fixed. We average about 45 mph on the highways.

We play 20 Questions in the car. It seems to me that every answer is "Bob Dylan," an animal, or the color red.

Knock knock. Who's there? Bob Dylan.

I talk about *The Magus,* the book I'm reading at the moment. Yeah, it's good, says Jon, but Hemingway is better. Faulkner is better, Steinbeck is better, Dostoevsky, Rimbaud is better. But that's pretty good.

Putting my head out the window to dry the sweat (no air-conditioning, hot summer) and get a good look at the desert—my Ray Bans (prized possession) fly off and bounce onto the shoulder. Pop refuses to stop.

Winslow, Arizona; a picnic on some dry dirt at the back of town, shade from one scraggly tree with a whole nation of ants. Watch the ants, industrious in the sweltering heat. We are all lifeless, limp. Disappointed because Winslow doesn't live up to the Jackson Browne song. ("It's a girl my lord in a flatbed Ford slowing down to take a look at me." Not so much glamour, really, in Winslow, in the long run.)

Zeke's blond curly locks and tiny barreled chest. He is always smiling, cracking jokes, getting into trouble, bouncing around, stubborn and strong as a mule. Joe is quiet and light-reflecting, like a miniature polar bear.

A hamburger joint in _____ . There is no such thing as fresh vegetables yet in this part of America. Choices: hamburger, tuna fish, grilled cheese, cottage cheese with pineapple. I'm fat and a vegetarian, so I always get the cottage cheese with pineapple. There is some scuffle under the table. Stop kicking me with your big boots you fucking oaf, says Pat. You fucking bitch. We kids wander off to the pool room.

Flagstaff; Pop gets sick. No one tells us why he is vomiting or shitting every five minutes, can barely move. Maybe he has the flu. We spend days wandering by the train tracks, nights at the campground. He goes to the doctor and gets a shot. Years later I learn that he nearly died that kick.

I have no consciousness, no idea like "this is difficult," "this is fucking difficult."

We are on the road again. More days go by in this manner.

Time is laid out in dark gloppy bands, like black clumps of glistening seaweed stretching both ways, forward and back, so that you can't tell where time ends or begins till someone comes along with a big shiny hatchet and lops off a piece into a segment of time—a doctor's appointment, a week, an afternoon.

Pagosa Springs, Colorado; we have made it to "the land," a small chunk of territory on the lower Rio Blanco, the only tangible thing to come out of the settlement ($3,000 of it), where Pat, Zeke and Jon will live in the trailer. But it rains all September and when the first snows hit in November, they move to Albuquerque and ditch the trailer. A few years later, some Pagosa Springs teenagers torch it, leaving a blackened radius in the scrub.

Sit next to my father on the stoop in front of the liquor store, yellow bug light flickering. What's wrong, he says.

I try to say something. What's wrong. I thought maybe you didn't love us. I say this. I was afraid you might think that, he says. He sounds annoyed with how obvious my statement is. That night he pulls Pat by the hair from the Chevy. "Are you happy now, little girl," she screams. We kids stay quiet in the tent.

Beda comes up to the land. They all drink beers, faces orange by the firelight.

I have sex on the hillside with a runaway on a motorcycle from Memphis with an orange bandana around his neck. Back home, there is a strict stepfather he doesn't like. We leave and he rides home, but calls me every few weeks for the next year or so, though I cannot remember what he looks like, his name. Joe remembers him slapping angrily at gnats.

When I get home I have a 105° fever and cannot talk for several days.

I tell this story to no one.

Years later, Joe tells me it was like his family dream—we were all together, however much things had run amok.

Interview
(Who is Asking / Who is Answering)

Pop, I'm writing a book about you. I mean, with you in it.
Are you ready to do this interview?

Mmrmph.

Okay, where were you in 1963?

In 1963, my father was 17 and clean clean clean as a whis-
tle. By 1968, I was three and he had descended into those
dark and distant lands called Heroin. The sun warming
his armpits in the afternoons.

What happens when that particular crystal gets slipped
into the vein?

A dark water into which the light descends only a short
distance, vestigial gill-slits emerge as the fluid colloid
pours in. A luminous, liquid night. Underwater, one can
think and dream. All our aqueous history laid out on the
sea-floor. In the emulsified dusk, one can see the strings
of a violin held down by eel-like pinkies. One can travel,
one can go.   (My father's early aquatic life is redeemed.)
The earth makes no light of its own, covered by a night's
pressure; what enemies here in the dark, what prey?
Sounds and color detach from their objects and float away.
Small invertebrates swim brightly through the blood-
stream. On the surface, under a full moon, the ship estab-

lishes a new weight. Sperm moves through body walls, all the tidal animals—no longer rooted to lunar waters—beams, flashes, fluctuating densities; the body moves back, pre-Cambrian, toward the Polychaete worms. We can organize disorderly things in the world, put public telephone receivers back in their cradles. These were the myths that invented feelings. We do not have to be afraid of heat, or of water, nor fire.

The Times I Have Wanted to Kick
My Father's Ass

The story he liked to tell about my mother's boyfriend Carl. Are you coming to the barbecue, Carl? Then why don't you bring a watermelon. My father says he and Carl understood each other, Carl was cool because Carl laughed. Everyone knows it's completely stupid to ask a Black person, your almost-ex-wife's boyfriend, if they are bringing a watermelon to a barbecue.

Every time he used the word "nigger" I wanted to kick his goddamn ass.

For every fight he tried to pick in a liquor store.

When he pulled his girlfriend by the hair from the Chevy in the dark up on the land even if she was being a royal bitch.

When, after I wrote "black stubs for teeth in his gums," he told me I had a fat ass.

Another Side of the Story:

For every racist comment, for every fag joke, there were also the times he fought or almost fought someone else who uttered the word "nigger." In either stance, shadow boxing some version of himself.

Early

I was conceived in the bushes on Sycamore Canyon Road. The result of that momentary folly was not just me, but a bad case of poison oak on the private parts of my parents-to-be. When we used to make the rare drive up the canyon to visit friends, long after my father was gone, my mother would point into the bushes and trees at a certain bend in the road, and say, "Look! That's where you were conceived."

The Primum Mobile

On the subway, I saw a man kiss the crown
of his

boy's head. A blister
is tenderness. I was always homesick for it, cigarettes

were no consolation. It's a question of the home-sound
about the hum, it's one
of electricity, each socket
in the house having its own destination and the appliances
all working in the night all

right—Like,

I would like to be inside the lights

of these peoples'
houses (with our ancient nostalgia for fire) but not

inside these lives.

Light Gathers About My People

Light comes through and is
beautiful, too; so
the eyes of my people. My people
are bounding across highways
toward buses to drive through beautiful American
backroads, humming, they are blind.

My people ride bicycles near freeways and handle guns badly, mouthing words with smoke rings moving into a dark, distant sky. My people laugh in the dark. They have no teeth in their mouths; so the smiles of their highly lit lighters. My people may be blind but my people have eyes in the backs of their heads. Wait! My people don't have any heads! My people, my people don't even know they are people! I replace my people with four-legged animals, they mewl around. Little bugs, they laugh again, antennae folding. I swap my people for cars, and now we can get there. I cash them in for a word of caution, now they can travel safe and stay where they are. I trade them for the stands of eucalyptus along the sides of the highway, for the sunlight that falls there, for what they traffic in. I trade them for everything they wanted to be, for cash-money converted and afternoon shade, for people who will greet me at the door, for the people they wanted to be and I wanted them to be here at this bend in the road with me.

The Land

What this has to do with is pipe-dreams. A man, my father, a nation of pipe-dreams. Enough pipe-dreams to fill up several countries, countries full of pipe-dreamers. I'm going to buy a big, beautiful piece of land near a rushing stream and build a big house out of stuff I find, like rocks and trees, leaves and mud to plug up the chinks, and you all can come live in it. There'll be a tunnel from one part to the next for privacy, we'll take saunas in the sweat-lodge and jump in the river. I'm thinking of starting a book-collecting business. I'm going to make a big pile of money on this next job and we'll all go to Greece, I'm going to carve faces into sticks and sell them to rich hippies, I'm going to set up a frog-catching business, as soon as I finish this novel, I'm going to write my autobiography, we're going to have crayfish for supper, I'm going to catch them down at the bosque with this hand-fashioned crayfish catcher.

Myth / Truth

Myth: Jon & my uncle Chris have a contract to play the music for *Easy Rider*. My dad takes a distinct disliking to Dennis Hopper ("He's a real asshole") and punches him in the nose.

Truth: They lose the recording contract. My dad did punch Dennis Hopper in the nose. Or my uncle did. Or a friend, or an acquaintance, or somebody they once heard about did.

Truth: My uncle moved to L.A. and was supposed to make an album under Hopper's tutelage.

Question: "What happened, Uncle Chris?"
Answer: "Uh, I got into a lot of trouble," he giggles. "Mostly drugs." (He doesn't mention the bullet still lodged near the base of his spine, which I think he got in Taos.)

Truth: There is a recording of my uncle singing "Easy Rider," based on Leadbelly's "CC Rider," in the film *American Dreamer*, or at least on the album of music from *American Dreamer*.

Question: Would my father and his brothers identify with the marshal (as played by Gary Cooper) in *High Noon*, or with the Miller Boys/bandits?

Of course, we all know the answer: bandits, bandits, bandits, those bad-ass boys were baby bandits.

Interview then Poem

— How did you survive?
— Survive what?
— How did you survive your father?
— There's nothing wrong with my father a little alcohol
and smack won't fix. What's that virus called, the one
where your insides rot and you puke your guts out? He
doesn't have that.

Essay (poem): Delicately

The father pollutes his body and
this is illegal and yet he does not
knowingly or purposefully pollute rivers
except by the small necessities
of daily living. Chevron pollutes rivers
and dirt and children are born
into brain cells in wrong places. If my father
smokes in a public place, this could
get him into trouble. If he shoots
heroin at home and someone
official finds him he
will be fined or arrested, maybe jailed.
This is the classic story in which a hero
sets out on a voyage, like Homer's or Dante's, and
along the way finds out something about
her/himself, only this time there's nothing
left to find out. For the world like Sappho was either

small, dark, and ugly
or small, dark, and beautiful.

Date Unknown
(Who is Talking / Who is Remembering)

The bird-like lights are hovering over Albuquerque where there is the easy living of Quonset hut casinos and the flashing blue circle of the Creamland sign near the abandoned transfer station.

Walking around the rim of his home, a 180-degree house, half the circumference of the volcano's vista, he says, if his life is a geological form, my father wishes for a place to step on all the edges of each red mesa and plateau where the rich dirt has piled up, he says

if I could thread these sides together
I would have a 360-degree home
a crater without seams, a center of *success*. Success lies in the layers of dirt, each one took hundreds upon hundreds of years to build up. If I dig here, I might find a flint-carved arrowhead that gleams at all of its edges, a place to build an underground room that is warm in the winter, cool in summer, and I could sweep the dirt off the floor right into the river.

Instead, I had $10 to get out of _____ de Navidad, tearing the door off its hinges in Teotihuacán and getting thrown in jail, mediocre out-of-body experiences ripping into muscle and pitching me against the wall. I've chickened out on all my visions—in my current state, I now have this clarity of mind: they were just bad pharmaceutical speed.

If there were a home to go home to, I'd go to San Ignacio, Widow's Tears (so-called because that stream dried up so fast each year); I'd get an extension on the story of my former life with creeks.

Red taillights slipping across the mesa, mountains rising out of the plain, winterfat bushes like chubby white wicks scrubbing up the dirt. Everybody wants to get home this Sunday night, greasy weekend feeling inside.

Is it my brother or is it my boyfriend or is it my father or my misbehaved baby driving across the scene?

Car taking off down 285, roaring like a jet.

A landscape so empty from certain angles that you yourself might feel totally emptied out, guts stored somewhere in the basement of some great desert palace in canopic jars.

Burnt as the piñon stumps out on the scrubland.

Because with nerves as jumpy as mine, ears as acute, world rolling like steam over my eyeballs, on which everything seems to stick—it's better to empty it all out.

Traffic lights ballooning out of the dark, opening like parachutes about to float off the face of the earth.

White houses sailing across brown, blind plains.

Towns in the distance out on the dark solid earth that look
like some alien ship came down out of the sky to set up
shop; then years later they abandon their little town—
they let the humans move in, and the humans said, Let's
call this Alamosa, Ft. Garland, Pueblo, Abiqui.

(Think up something new to say about stars.)
The stars look like they're about to pass out.
Pass out, and on to another plane.
(Has somebody already said that?)

We make enough plastic wrap in America each year to
shrink wrap the state of Texas. Say something about that
and stars.

Tenebrific stars, believed to cause night.

Jon says, I'll say:
I guess the sun's going down in its right place.
      Or:
The sun's going down five inches off tonight—missed its
proper spot—a little drunk I guess! drunk sun!

Truth lies in the mind.
The eye brought it there and buried it, what it saw.

Small angers we hold transparent to reason like pieces of
sharp-edged ice that never melt but float in the body, trav-
el through lungs and liver and kidneys, settle about the
heart, blind augers; that's history. Shards nearly as pol-
ished as beach glass over time, but wicked enough to rip

open a vein now and again. What are they? What formed them? The night your mother screamed at your father and you heard all the words, how your father shook your hand when you returned from ten months in Europe. What angers and deceits, what disappointments and rages, weaknesses, let in the small latches that would later make the whole thing unhinge?

What is the moral framework of this piece?
Piece of what?
Writing? Life?

The moral is not forgive and forget (though in this story neither is a moral lapse). The moral is the story, and the story is a life. The life said

A Carnet for Popsicle

Does or does
not an event
have a position
in space? Here
is an event:
My father is splashing
his toes in the
water.

His toe-
nails grow

greedy. In the somber & emotionally
repressed environment of his portion of
historical America, does
or does it not
have to do with
craters
aethers
that blue
shirt blue
cap of that
kind of beer, bus
transfer,
shade, crack-
pipe, Naltrexone & oh
shade, that
Turquoise
Lodge sleigh

ride shade thing. Light
might not be able to turn the corner

of the street, but my
father turns
corners on more streets than I
can keep track of. Just as they were trying to set a limit
(boundary)
to light, he turns again. But
if I name light, like looking
at a direct light (sun) I also name pain. At the happy
appearance of color, if I put light
at the back of his knees, he will dream. These are lights
from lamps and
maps and elsewhere.
All the

beauty of all the
light
blue finds itself in
Eu-

clid. Is it my dad or light that gives
from black to white? The dark is rough, the light
is smooth, but the weight of light is like

with ants.
With light, the waters become

laughier. At the interior of the body
is black
with light organized into what parts? They say hell is

it intensified. In what light

cannot do or undergo, excluding
light; that can be stopped or skirted or self-
propagated; Let's call this
Rays of Light; lights form as light
formats itself from what was previously

non-light. Does not give us objects but
their shadow, from black to
this scene: indivisible, invisible, to make

the visible seen. In the future
light-
cone of the
event called
past-

light, we will have these
spectra red-shif-
ted (Move
toward me) Who will, blue? (Move
away.) Here is my forward, here is my
back. What light says I can't

say The sym-
metry of
light
like stars
at night
versus
stars

in the day. What can we do in dark hours? Abstain?
In the bright we can say

What space, what verge, what amplitude
of the little light like gods' droplets, "rainbow proofs
on the roof"

An Inventory of Jon's Visions I Know About (Dream Events)

—Owl with a 60-foot wing span flits over the highway at Tres Piedras

—Ghosts arrive in carriages for a high-class tea in an orchard

—Enormous ponies crossing the road to Chama

—Devils and ghouls and the generally dead busting through doors in Mexico City

Date Un

If I can just not do anything for a few moments so that I can think about my father; cease all activity except the concentration of the plane taking off, and think about my father; the father speeding away in the dark below, under the blackened clouds of Albuquerque, cumulus shot through with orange and pewter; he himself speeding only when someone else is at the helm. Otherwise, shambling. He shambles around through the underbrush of Albuquerque. His camp is no longer near the dumpsters, but in a pile of wood chips between University and the War Zone (high crack area). On the other side of Albuquerque, in the neighborhood and house in which he used to live, the city seems harmless, quiet. But circling his camp are men with crow bars and tire irons and guns, hiding in dark corners of the road and in alleyways. You need a Road Dog, he told me, a partner wise in the ways of the street, to watch your back. Jon has recently had his head smashed in, and the wounds became gangrenous. In the hospital, he was given hot oatmeal in the morning and pudding after dinner. He could bathe, and his sheets were clean. Each day he thought up new ailments, but they soon released him. He left the pale blue plastic band fluttering nostalgically on his wrist for weeks.

It is wearying to write about my father the big-bad-drug-gie-with-gun-dabblings-guy over and over. I'm tired of the brilliantly-talented-tortured-father sometimes-mean-guy persona on him. I know this fatigue to be because I saw him today and there before me was my father. His chest

was thin. I would like him to find another woman, or
rather for her to find him, and make a family of him again
(but no more children!). That woman would bathe him,
dress him in clean clothes and feed him, put him in a warm
house and lay him down in a warm bed, and lay down with
him, too, so that he, my father, might make it to 60, or 68—
enough years for us to see him, and for all of us to grow big.
It is possible that he might use that woman up, that her
life would be spent with it, the years of looking after his
socks, and waiting for him to come home, taking care of
him when he crashes the truck, or gets hit with a crowbar
to the head. It might no longer be possible, after fifteen
years with that man, for that woman to tank up and drive.
Or it may be that her life will have gained some small
thing, a grain of understanding or feeling about the
humans who live here; or perhaps some big thing, some
grid of understanding that connects hearts and their atti-
tudes and bodies and astronomy, physics and dust and cry-
ing babies and zoo animals and fiber optics, thereby.

Clouds / H

Someone else is driving. My father and I are lying in the back of the truck looking up at the clouds. He is describing all the animal shapes he sees, and all the animals he's ever known. There is, for a moment, nothing that separates us. "Have you ever tried H," he asks. This was a clean period, a stretch of seven years in which he only chipped, using once or twice a year. He begins to speak of it as someone might speak of a lover. "She's the lady who turns the heavens, the Wheel of Fortune, the ninth sphere, the first circle of Hell . . ." His voice droned on and on but I had already frozen and contracted as the space between us grew. He was drifting, in memory, back up to the clouds.

The Greeks had stories to explain how whole houses, ancestral lines, rise and fall. No mother I know of in our history served up her own children at a feast, but there is some stain like that rose marking the House of Atreus. We are descended from noblemen, Venetian counts, Nobel-nominees, Mayflower pilgrims, a detective in the Scotland Yard (who snoozed while some queen was shot), and morphine addicts. For my father and his brothers were not the first nor the last with this fierce hawk on their shoulder. My father's grandfather was a doctor, trained at Bellevue, who was sent to the sanatorium every year to dry up. There are likely many versions of the story, but one I was told is that my great grandmother found him in the closet on his last morphine dose, tourniqueted and dead.

Some day I will be able to write of how the disease dropped

down into my generation, like a fire jumping a ditch and raging through the next line of trees, and my father's role in that; but not this day.

What I Left Out

What did I leave out? What should I put in? The crazy aunt (my mother's sister) with whom my father had an affair when I was three or four? All the nasty details of a life gone awry? If it is not about confessions, about cathar- sis, what is it about? I only have this thin slice on the life: it is from a daughter's eye. I have forgotten to put in not the most lurid details, but the most beautiful curves in an hour or a minute—because his voice is coming through a thick fog, because from here I can't call up the movement of his hands.

Objects too Heavy for Earth

When you are a drowning man, you need things that float. How can I explain this? For some people, all the objects of the world lose buoyancy; they pull you down. Bus schedules, chainsaws, belts, wallets, money, socks, liquor stores, trees—like lead weights around the wrists and ankles. You are moving through a vast lawless land of watery air. Gravity has new rules. A coffee cup is like a sinking freighter in your hand. My father was a fine swimmer; it was the world that got too heavy—a trick of science, like that water separated into its heaviest parts, or all the dark matter, the unknown weight of the universe, gathered in everything you touch.

Unfinished Poem that Keeps Trying to Write Itself as if Written by Jon

Hey, caballero, I said
to the sparrow
fancy-throated boy
dancing on the banks
of the Seine
thuggy caballero stealing crumbs

Ay, compañero
I said to the sparrow
you lazy little dancer
eyeing cake scraps all morning
without offering me any
of your dusty dress of feathers

Hey, caballero, come

The Last Book He Told Me

One day, when he was living in Arroyo Seco up in the mountains above Taos, my father and his friends got very hungry. They had eaten nothing but bread for some days. So down they went to Valdez, where they knew a farmer had some sheep. They crept over the mocassined earth, soil thick and spongy beneath their feet. Up he grabbed a little lamb and tucked it into his armpit, Jon and the lamb, running across the dirt. But when he got to the fence, he looked at the lamb hard in the face and knew he could never eat it, and said (or at least he says he said), Why, er, excuse me, sir, to the small lamb thing in his arms, and walked it slowly back to its original square footage, set it down, and instead found the henhouse and grabbed up two chickens, which, at home, he half plucked and boiled, but those damn hens were bitter as could be.

BOOK OF THE DEAD

The possibility of illusion is a by-product of our cognitive architecture, to be sure, and falsehood is as much the dark companion of truth as death is of life.

— ARTHUR C. DANTO

*A man is a golden impossibility. The line he must walk
is a hair's breadth.*

RALPH WALDO EMERSON

A dream all afloat, or, more accurately, drowning. And everywhere I walked, more pools and puddles and lakes and swamps, for a drowning. Blue, blue and sinking. But that is not the dream I will think of tonight.

For us humans, it's real when a person dies. Life has ended. It is a life that belonged to a person, a body, someone we loved. But whose life is it? It does not feel so much like a life has ended, but life itself, in some unknown quantity and mix; it may be my own. "The human career is long," it passes from one human to the next. I went through it in all the languages I know. My father is dead.

This morning, the cat interpreted my father's death for me. The whole theatre was running through her; she was like a TV, but you couldn't see the show, not in pictures; you could see it by means of electricity and heat.

Leading up to my father's death, every time I called his ex-wife, we used to play a little game: Is he dead yet? No, she would say, not yet, and there was a small relief. He wasn't dying, he was drunk. When the phone rang Saturday morning, it was my brother, and I was happy to hear his voice.

I Will Not Go to Space

I will not go to space
in your rusty rocket "that rests
on coral waves" deeply
deeply golden in the frangible glass

Golden, you kill me
with your little mungo things, in the "Is he
dead yet?" game. For us humans, it's real
when a cat interprets that death. That cat
doesn't know we're not married, nor
what we are, shiny beads for eyes, little qua qua
of the ordinary legs
of ordinary women, and the men
who love them, them
ordinary legs, and the women who do

Golden, five million flowers' worth per pint
of honey to the left or to the right
of the sun; the translucent white gloves
of ghosts of larval bees tell the story
of an idling memory of a friend's house
in flames. We extinguish it. But when the soul's
on fire, add kindling. But, golden,
break my glasses, sip this folding golden
whiskey, let the talkies
of Kevin Costner get blurry in our minds, tan-
colored pretzels battling
over the batter's stand as the sun sets over the West
and western clouds on
Dog's Neck. Nothing prepares us for death.

Three Dreams + His Belongings

Three dreams occurring simultaneously, so that it is hard to untangle the threads (note that the mind is capable of staging three stories at once).

We live in a homestead in Wisconsin or Wyoming, which seems to be, geographically, in California's spot. Jon has been in some kind of traffic accident and is going to die. Or, Jon has some kind of illness (alcoholism and drug addiction, in truth), and if he takes care of himself, perhaps he will not die. Us kids barrel out, racing toward town, across a long, lazy stretch of prairie with tall (tall as our heads), golden-yellow grass. Behind us, where the house is, a string of high, blue mountains. The racing is in play at first, but soon becomes serious—a race for help, someone to save my father—as the oldest brother, tow-headed, chases us back and then turns around toward town again. We all follow and he chases us back again, and I am stumbling through the weeds, my brown knees going up and down, and I am scared now.

Simultaneously: as adults, we are swimming in a deep, endless irrigation ditch—also headed to town for help—and I am wondering which one of is strong enough to swim the whole way, whose arms are strong enough to knock Jon out—Joe? No. Me? No. Chris? Maybe. Poppy? No. I wish Laird was here.

Simultaneously: Jon back at the homestead, being sick. A rip in the fabric of the rug.

Simultaneously, in the doublefold of this third part of the dream, is the corner where the accident took place, a busy mountain thoroughfare, and a tear through the concrete, which we must repair.

The children arrive at the general store, out of breath.

A plump older woman in a flower-print sackcloth dress, apron around her waist, grey hair in a bun, etc., comes out. What is it, child?
We need a rug to fix up the accident, we say, panting.
She bustles inside to look for rugs. It seems there are several to choose from. Our plan is to throw the rug over the scrape marks and then paint it black. But which scrape— the one in the house, or the one at the corner? The old woman comes back. Does Laird know, child, so he can help you? she asks. Why, if it's for outside, take this smaller rug here—she points to a rectangular white throw rug hanging on a clothesline in the corner. You won't need anything fancy for that.

The inside tear that needs repairing; the outside one (the more reparable face of the world). But no one is strong enough to save Jon.

Book of Dreams
(as collected by Eleni & Pat)

Dear Pat,

I had a dream that your friend, my dad, Jon was a seri-
al killer—which is why they bumped him off—but then
it was not certain that he was really the culprit, so the
law brought him back from the dead (isn't that just like
the law?), and he was stooping around the stove in his
bent-shouldered, bent-kneed way, saying, "They said I
wh-whhat? Oh, no c'mon, guys, you know I didn't do
that . . ."

And meanwhile, in real life, he is still riding around in
my suitcase in a plastic bag (ashes). I am waiting to get
to Delphi, and maybe Lefkada and/or Santorini. Or do
you think it's better not to scatter him in too many
places, seeing as he was so scattered in life?
(ELENI, 4/20/00)

A dream about Jon in which he showed me what he was
up against. Or Jon and his bootstraps. We had been
hanging out most of the day, and then we were in a box-
car-like thing, a train maybe but smaller like a dump-
ster, and it was the end of the day and Jon was showing
me what he had to do next. Long flat things were laid on
top of other long flat things, and he had to get to the bot-
tom of the pile while he was standing on it. And so he

reached down with one hand to lift and move stuff while leaning on the wall with the other hand and trying to jump or levitate above the stuff which was all piled underneath him every which way, and of course it was impossible to get his boots and his weight off the pile for long and when he came back down on the boards it flattened his hand under it. And he looked at me indicating that the stuff was his and had to be dealt with on a regular basis. I must also add that the box had plenty of light in it, and was not dirty.

(CHRIS, 3/16/00)

The important thing was, I woke up with the same feeling as when Jon was alive and the day held a sort of promise, a promise of adventure. If he woke up before you did, it was going to be a day. He'd wake you up, and he'd be smoking cigarettes and drinking coffee and already thinking about something. It was just a memory of how, let's see, what would be the word, I don't know, it was sort of exhilarating or something to be hanging out with Jon. Because everything seemed like it held some sort of promise when I was with him. What else? I don't know how to describe it but it was the sort of feeling that life was mysterious but it could be figured out. Everything had the potential of being understood. When I would hang out with Jon everything was sort of an adventure, and when I woke up, it felt like I had just had an adventure with him.

(POPPY, 3/18/04)

so i've had this dream about daddy, i've had it like three times, it's not a descriptive dream but. he had to come back (from the dead, or wherever) to give me this book he had written about me and him (him and i?), and whenever he starts to hand me the book, he disappears. and then that's the end of the dream, but i've had this same dream seriously 3 times.

(POULI, 1/18/03)

as you ask for Jon Dreams I am Complying by sending some of my memories of Jon . . . . early remembering . . . . . . listen to music on . . . . by Bob Dylan at that stage of my life
The sounds of the voice and the music . . . wondrous topics . . . there on the . . . at that house with those people . . . the music . . . the Jon . . . the Chris . . . the son and on . . . where and when you're . . . been with the Bald mother the Daughter of Southern my the sound heard own voice pipe in lyric recurring . . . the music the music . . . with me . . . Dreams about

(MELITSA, 3/15/04)

Had a dream about Pop last night where he was rehearsing for a tough guy role in some movie or play we were doing. He was walking around nervously, menacingly, and flexing the muscles in his temples the way he used to (I guess by grinding his teeth) when I was a kid. He was asking if it was effective, and some-

one—maybe you or Pat—was saying, no, it wasn't really.
(JOE, 3/29/04)

All of my dreams about Jon have the same basis: he is still alive, but unaware of his coming death. I'm trying to tell him that he can avoid it, but he always just nods slowly and shows a lazy grin, but it's clear that what I'm telling him has no effect on him, and I can't change his course.

The most recent dream, on 09/29, Jon's birthday: the sky is midnight blue and I am in the presence of Jon. It's dark, but the sun and the moon are both shining brightly in the sky. I'm talking to him, but he's not there in physical form. The urgency of my message increases as the sun and the moon move across the sky, and just as I'm reaching the climax of my speech to him, the sun and the moon cross paths in a beautiful colorful eclipse, and it's all over.
(ZEKE, 9/29/?)

Pat,

You and I were working in a salt mine—a big 19th-century atrium high on a rock outcropping—shoveling up salt crystals, big transparent lead-grey stones, which we piled into a wheelbarrow. The air was dense and steamy, and the windows were fogged over with salt and grime and sweat. You went into a small back room to dig, and I went to help, but when I opened the door, there was Jon's body in a bathtub, with a cloudy halo seeping out into the water. You had found him (maybe in a refrigerator), and carried him there. I stepped out fast, and said I couldn't work in there with him. "Why?" you asked, "too scary?" "Yeah, and he stinks." So you picked him up in your arms, and carried him, dripping, back into the main room. We continue to dig and pile salt crystals into wheelbarrows while the windows steam up more. Jon is lying on the ground behind us. And then he says something. Some gruff comment on what we've been doing, in a deep, low voice, and we turn, and you kneel by him. His stomach and legs shudder, and he says more, kind of sassy stuff. He has been in a deep catatonia, from drinking, not really dead. But changed. Not exactly human. There's a kind of excitement—perhaps these six weeks (it was six in the dream) of deathlike slumber have taught him something, have made him decide to stop drinking, to come to life in a new way. I wake, I fall asleep again. Jon is still lying there, the room is spinning, and this song sings itself:

Indigo, Indigo,
Where in the world do you want to go?
What city, what state, what country, what world?

And a list of all the things Jon could be in being born back into the world appeared.

Rock
Salt
Truck

Scissors
Grass
Bird
Spider
Paper
Frog
Oak
Rubberband
Whirligig
Etc.

(ELENI, DATE UNKNOWN)

Here's What I Want:

"A little house out in the fields. A little house out on the plains and nothing but grasses all around and in the distance that great mountain range that rises where two continents bit into each other. But I accidentally sold the Rio Blanco land and used all the money on drugs."

Light like a fly buzzing around his wrist

He is at that underground banquet in which animals act as humans.
Great bulls playing the lyre.
Lions singing songs.
A jackass telling the tale.
In this golden trench, all the animals once living can trade stories, thoughts, limbs, faces, heads.

My father, a thing wrapped by cushiony earth and time.

It was hard for him to shake youth; hard to get rid of the notion that he could do anything; a man who would forever be 20 or 30 in his mind; not psychologically rigged for middle-age.

I would like to think it was that stupidity—the flood of it around him in men and women under the sway of money and time—the drowning stupidity Gustave Flaubert found all around him and despaired of—that made my father decide to step off the dark curb and out of the world. But in fact his hatred of that stupidity corrupted him so that he himself became stupid—too stupid to live.

Dante's love wouldn't work for my father for, as it turned out, my father was a real man, an object in corporeality, in real time.

(one page) Three
When she

I know she walks the chair around
The couch

She talks out loud of
course points her feet
gears up gears down
and when she gets
loose enough to joke
on the phone with
one hand you can
god damn bet she
kick a murderers heart
around in a little
wooden bot (3x5)

...e is the list of his belongings, as compiled by the office
...f Public Health:

2 packs cigarettes (both opened, one pack Camels, one
pack Marlboros)
2 black combs
5 books matches
3 pairs glasses (one for reading, two 1970s-looking sun-
glasses with big frames)

Also in this envelope with his belongings but not listed on the outer label, a receipt for the De Anza Motor Lodge, Room 152, for which he paid $33.10, cash. He checked in on January 5, 2000 with one other person, a man. He did not check out. When the hotel manager, Amir, opened the door to Room 152 on January 7th, he found my father on the floor, "sleeping."

In a separate manila envelope is the money in my father's possession, the amount marked in pencil on the outside: $11.42.

Those were the things that belonged to my father on the last day of his life. No wallet. No pictures. No home address.

The De Anza Motor Lodge is at 4301 Central, in Albuquerque, New Mexico. The hotel manager is an immigrant from Tanzania. As a young man, he was one of the 45,000 East Indians and Pakistanis expulsed from Uganda by Idi Amin. He emigrated from Tanzania to Albuquerque fifteen years ago. Every evening, from 7:00 to 9:30 P.M., he attends church, and so was not at the front desk when my father checked in. About midnight, he says, he saw the two men from Room 152 in the parking lot, "maybe drunk," most likely high as lords.

A mysterious presence holds the only information about my father's last minutes. His road dog, Little John, has the word out on the street, and even the bike cops, who had a certain fondness for my crazy father, are keeping their ears open to find out who checked into the De Anza Motor Lodge with my father that night.

The young thanatologist who performed the autopsy, Dr. Klein, cites several possible causes of death. The patient had an enlarged heart, serious liver disease. He had in his possession Xanax and clozapine (indicated for the management of "severely ill" schizophrenic, bipolar, depression and dementia patients "who fail to respond adequately to standard antipsychotic drug treatment"). (Clozapine is known to carry a "significant risk of [causing] seizures"; up to a one week supply may be provided to the patient to be held for emergencies, such as "weather, holidays.")

Jon had also recently been prescribed:

Forms of CARBAMAZEPINE (Clinical indications: seizure disorders; non-FDA approved to stabilize various mood disorders. Abrupt withdrawal may precipitate status epilepticus)

CARBATROL (a carbamazepine) (Potential dose-related side effects include: drowsiness, diplopia, headache, ataxia, nausea, vomiting, dizziness. Other systemic side effects include: abdominal pain, constipation, diarrhea, loss of appetite. Rare but potentially life-threatening reactions to all forms of carbamazepine involve aplastic anemia, toxic hepatitis, and pancreatitis)

DILANTIN (an antiepileptic drug related in chemical structure to the barbiturates)

DEPAKOTE (prescribed for epilepsy and manic episodes; "typical symptoms of mania include pressure of speech, motor hyperactivity, reduced need for sleep, flight of ideas, grandiosity, poor judgement, aggressiveness, and possible hostility")

The alcohol level in his blood might have been deadly. It is possible that, for the first time in two years, he had missed his methadone dose. (Little John reports that there was some trouble with the dosing nurse that day.) He might have had a brain seizure. His heart (in some traditions believed to be a seat of consciousness) may have jolted then stopped. It may have been, if it were a crack-cocaine overdose, a very painful death: my father clutching at his head and pounding himself against the walls till he falls to the floor, limbs jolting, then twitching. We do not wish this. The living hope that the dead did not suffer at the moment of dying. We hope that a small spot of dimness appeared on the horizon and spread slowly, peacefully covering the eyes, blanketing each spinning thought till the lights go out. Having seen his eldest daughter and estranged son recently, he might have decided that all was in order. He might have simply sighed and stopped breathing. He might have been, after twenty-eight years of intermittent drug use and alcoholism, very tired. There were no signs of trauma to the body.

One day a person is on this side of the world with you, and you can think of that person walking down a quiet, s street, or you can think of calling them, or of them ca you, even if they haven't called you in years, and of what you might say to each other, all the interesting ideas of late; he might tell you in great detail about his dream of people living in tunnels and caves in a large mountain, and his step-sister the poet was there; and you can think of going to visit him, in his town, and of seeing him standing in the kitchen in the middle of the night in his underwear, knees bent slightly, hands (as always) dangling at the ends of his arms; and of his deep, rough and deeply comforting smell of tobacco smoke and woodchips. And then, one day, that person is no longer on this side of the world with you. There is a thin veil, a flimsy partition, and this person, a person you love, has stepped across it and off into the dark world. He is dead.

And I can no longer imagine visiting him in this world. I can imagine very little, really, maybe nothing, about the black place into which he has crossed. It is unfathomable that I will, for the present, continue my life on this side of it—the side of days and nights, and pigeons, bagels with butter, and sunlight. What is he doing on the other side? Is he doing something? Or nothing? I can imagine him in his old world only, the one I am in now; or not really even in this one, but in pictures of this one, from a former time; pictures of him doing something in the past, something I have seen him do or can imagine he would have done; but no pictures of him now—no pictures of how his face might have changed, of what new thoughts he has conceived, no trajectory of life lived and the person who goes along changing to fit that life.

I see my father in his underwear—dingy white briefs, sagging in the butt; he is standing in the kitchen in front of the refrigerator, bathed in the refrigerator's grey light, his left hand on the refrigerator door, knees bent slightly so that he looks as though he's lurching forward or back, right hand dangling chimpanzeelike at the end of its arm.

"I long to see my mother standing in the doorway," wrote Grace Paley.

I long to see my father standing in the hallway, by the refrigerator in the middle of the night, I long to see him on the stoop, in this world, not in dreams; I long to be able not just to converse, but even to imagine conversing with him, hunkered down in the backyard dust, in the future.

I see my father standing in the kitchen. He is fully clothed but his clothes are dirty and he is very thin. This is a real scene, a scene dragged up from this world, an actual past. The orange juice is too rich, he's been too broke to buy it, he waters it down from the tap. I cook him eggs and toast and wash his clothes for him while he takes a shower and then we sit in the backyard on the paving stones in the dust and he swishes his toes back and forth as we talk and sometimes leans over to scratch his feet—they are eerily pale, like some damp fishes that live in deep caves deprived of sunlight.

Before me stands a young boy in a Cub Scouts uniform, cradling a cat in his arms. He is looking shyly up into my eyes (but not my grandmother's eyes, as she holds the camera), into the sunlight. He is full of sweetness, full of potential.

Before me stands a boy of sixteen. He has just been to the Louvre for the first time in his life, and he has a little bit of a painting in his pocket—a small black hair of Rousseau's paintbrush, and the thin coat of black paint over it, which he has pulled from a painting he fell for, and could not imagine living without. The boy keeps this tiny piece for years and years in his pocket, fingering it until there is nothing left but a pinch of sand.

Before me is my father, up to his old self, circa his mid-twenties, sitting in an old Chevy, full of an unboundable energy that fairly ripples under his skin. He steps out of the truck, broad-chested and towering (much taller than he was in life), strong as anything. He has accidentally bonked his head on the truck door, and that's what will send him reeling into sickness and stupor—and then I realize that he is going to die.

Some days it disturbs me—some days it deranges every cell in my body—that my father died homeless, thin, coughing, in dirty clothes, in a cheap motel, in a wretched state where a glass of orange juice was an unbearable luxury.

In Dante's conception of the world, we see only a sliver of ourselves here on Earth; the rest of it is ghostly or heavenly, haunting us. Or we are ghosts here on earth, shadows of our full selves. Only when we bust free of this world can we find the one hundred percent.

I see my father in his underwear, in a huge dark space with brilliant lights, and the black is bluish and textured behind its darkness, and the lights are as of an enormous city that we cannot quite see—just its golden, glowing lights; and the buildings are wider and higher than the mind can conceive, going up and up, uncovered and covered in fog, and over the top, the lights are the lights of stars going off, shooting and sailing into the dark sky, like rockets.

Deaths / Funerals
The Albuquerque Tribune

SIKELIANOS—Jon Peter Steven Sikelianos, son of Glafkos and Marian Sikelianos, lumberjack poet, musician extraordinaire, and tree doctor, died Thursday, January 6, in Albuquerque. Born in New York, Jon grew up in a bohemian whirl of places, including Cape Cod, Santa Barbara, and Lausanne, Switzerland, and with a variety of cats and dogs and birds, including Cooniebally and Shag. Fisherman, boat builder, lover of animals, seer of ghosts, pocket knife collector, cigarette lighter thief, eater of unpaid-for peaches at Landmark, oatmeal maker, good cook, teller of dog stories (among which were the Purple Dog and the mischievous Tufeley and Drakely), hand-carved canemaker, singer of many children's songs, Jon was able to play just about any musical instrument he put his hand to. His tools of choice were guitar and piano, but he also played banjo and chainsaw. In his 20s, Jon learned the art of tree climbing, and became an expert tree surgeon, who specialized in climbing 100-foot tall eucalyptus, and in shaping trees to their most elegant forms. His sense of balance was perfected to a graceful performance rigged somewhere high above the skyline. Koala-like, coatimondi-like, Kodiak-bear-like, gorilla-like, Jon could often be found raiding the refrigerator in the middle of the night, or snapping his toes, reading one of his hundred-per-week-quota books on the porch, despite taped-together glasses and a column of ash building on the end of his cigarette. Jon worked at several zoos, from which he gathered many tales about Boufa the Russian bear, and from which he would sometimes bring home animals to visit. Christmas presents he gave his children include Jimi Hendrix's "The Cry of Love," zebra finches, a red '78 of Leadbelly singing "All the Children Get So Happy on a Christmas Day," panda figurines, and a Tonka crane. He gave three of his children their first guitars. Over the course of his life, Jon had many plans, which included: becoming a bookseller, collecting precious woods to build guitars and violins, becoming an expert frog-catcher, and chronicling all the creeks he'd ever known, beginning with the San Ysidro. Some of Jon's favorite songs included "Good Night Irene," "Freight Train" and "Takes a Lot to Laugh, Takes a Train to Cry." In sandwich hugs, he usually played the part of the bread. He is survived by four siblings, Mark, Chris, Melitsa and Poppy Sikelianos; by his four children, and their mothers.

LIST OF PHOTOGRAPHS